THE

OVERTHINKER'S

GUIDE TO JOY

THE
OVERTHINKER'S
GUIDE TO JOY

*A Handbook
for Overachievers,
People-Pleasers, and
Perfectionists*

JACKIE DE CRINIS

Host of *The Overthinker's Guide to Joy* podcast

JdC

Press

Maui, Hawaii

JdC Press

JdC Press
Maui, Hawaii, United States
Copyright © 2024 by Jackie de Crinis. All rights reserved.

Library of Congress Control Number: 2024920146

Paperback ISBN: 979-8-9909520-0-3
eBook ISBN: 979-8-9909520-1-0
Audiobook ISBN: 979-8-9909520-2-7

Book cover and interior design by Erin Seaward-Hiatt
Editorial production by KN Literary Arts

To my dad, who always laughed at my stories and told me I should write them down.

To my mom, who left this world too soon but remains my guardian angel and guiding light every day.

CONTENTS

INTRODUCTION

I've always wanted to write a self-help book because I am a massive fan of this genre.

I have stood in the aisles of bookstores for countless hours, combing through titles and book covers and reading a few chapters before deciding on my "purchase du jour."

My home library is filled with self-help books dating back to the early 1980s. But to be honest, despite my love of the genre, I find most self-help books too technical and overwritten.

While the titles usually hold great promise or offer at least one golden nugget of insight, they are often repetitive and tend to bury you in graphs and pie charts.

I understand that many self-help books are written by researchers who have conducted experiments to prove their hypotheses.

It's true, I don't have an MD, PhD, MFT, or MSW to add to my name. My academic journey took a different turn, leading me to a BA in psychology after a failed attempt at a pre-med track in college. More on that later.

Despite all those missing letters after my name, I've come to realize that there is no better way to understand overthinkers than to spend thirty years in the television industry—which I did. This unique perspective combined with my second career as a life coach has inspired me to write this book for *overthinkers*, *people-pleasers*, and *perfectionists*, like me, who want to feel less anxious and be happier and healthier.

The television industry provided me with an excellent education. It gave me insight into corporate America, Fortune 500 companies, red-carpet events, first-class travel, fancy hotels, retreats, and fine dining, and introduced me to countless interesting people—including a ton of celebrities.

However, it's an industry that doesn't care about the personal toll it takes on your life, and my day-to-day work life was a far cry from the glamorous world of limos, award shows, and expense accounts. The entertainment business expects you to eat, breathe, and sleep your job; and being a woman in a male-dominated industry is always an extra challenge. Women are often made to feel they should be grateful for even having a seat at the table. I accepted things like:

- the man-splaining
- unwanted sexual innuendos
- returning to work after only six weeks of maternity leave for fear of losing my job

Or going the extra mile, such as:

- commuting an hour each way in bumper-to-bumper traffic

- working a full day in the office and then being on the sets of sitcoms until after midnight several nights a week
- managing bosses who would bark orders only to change their minds on a whim
- reading and watching endless amounts of material every day of the week . . . including weekends
- working on every vacation

The entertainment industry is rife with self-promoters, con artists, glad-handers, opportunists, narcissists, and actual deviants. But it has also nurtured some of the greatest artists, storytellers, and exciting individuals I have ever met. Many have remained close friends, and several became my coaching clients.

But while I was working in the industry, my stress level was through the roof, and my nervous system was always in overdrive. I attempted to manage my stress by seeing a parade of chiropractors, acupuncturists, talk therapists, massage therapists, physical therapists, and a whole host of medical doctors.

But none of it really helped.

I still suffered from chronic headaches, muscle tension, digestive issues, insomnia, and anxiety. I didn't know how to relax, unwind, or unplug. I lived in a constant state of go-go-go!

I have always been a hard worker. This quality made me a reliable, trustworthy, dedicated, and passionate executive. One might say I was a Motivated Mindy. However, after years of being the dependable, hardworking, can-do-it-all girl without boundaries and healthy habits,

I went from being a Motivated Mindy to a Burned-Out Betty.

After working in television for thirty years, I decided to take a gap year for myself since I had never taken the opportunity as a teenager. My objective of that year was not to travel or hang out but to figure out what I wanted to do in the next chapter of my life. I wanted to return to helping people instead of just entertaining them. In addition, I aimed to learn how to calm my nervous system and live a more holistic and balanced life. My goal was to learn to love and appreciate my life, career, and, most importantly, myself.

I started taking courses and reading about everything that interested me, including meditation, nutrition, yoga, writing, psychology, and life coaching.

Life coaching was the career path that allowed me to incorporate everything I studied and loved. More importantly, it allowed me to help others.

Now, I coach overthinkers, people-pleasers, and perfectionists to embrace self-care and mindfulness to combat stress and burnout. Throughout my life, I always wanted a handbook to help me manage my overthinking brain and chronic anxiety.

So, I decided to create my own.

This book is not intended to replace proper medical attention in case of a serious medical or mental health issue. It's simply a compilation of daily routines and tools I suggest to my clients to reduce anxiety and live a healthier, happier life.

This book was written from a lifetime of experience as a wife, mother, corporate executive, and as a life coach.

At the age of fifty-five, I started meditating, blogging, podcasting, and coaching. I have just turned sixty, and this is my first book. So, if nothing else, please remember: *You're not broken, you're not too old, and it is never too late to start living the life you want . . . instead of just surviving the one you have.*

Happy reading!

CHAPTER 1

Running on Empty

It was December of 2004, and I'd just returned to work from maternity leave following the birth of my third child. My brain was still foggy from sleep deprivation and baby brain, a common syndrome for postpartum moms. On my first day back in the office, I was slammed with a full day of meetings. There was no easing back into the workday.

It was the last meeting of the day, around five. It was already dark outside. Two writers were coming in to pitch a storyline for a project that I had bought before going on maternity leave.

I was a big fan of one of the writers, but I didn't realize she wasn't planning on doing the writing for this project. She was going to supervise her husband, an unknown writer. It was a kind of a bait and switch, and I was not happy.

The husband did most of the talking, and I had trouble following along. Although I had sat through hundreds of story pitches in my career, I could not track what he was talking about.

My mind started racing.

What was wrong with me? Why couldn't I grasp what he was saying? How could I engage in this conversation without looking like an idiot? Why had I bought this project in the first place?

Suddenly, I noticed a slight chemical smell coming from the ventilation system. It felt like someone had turned off the air conditioning. I was worried that I was going to pass out from the lack of oxygen. I looked around the room, but no one else seemed to be bothered.

I didn't want to draw attention to my sudden paranoia and discomfort, so I politely nodded my head and asked a few generic questions. Finally, I said, "Let's discuss this with our team and get back to you with our thoughts."

When the writers left, I asked my colleagues, "Was I the only one confused? Or did the pitch make sense to you?"

They admitted it was a convoluted story pitch, but they weren't sure what to add to the conversation. I felt a modicum of relief. At least I wasn't losing my mind. Unfortunately, I realized I had bought a dud of a project, but that was another issue.

Then I asked, "Did you guys notice a weird smell, and did someone turn off the air in the building?" They shook their heads no.

Suddenly, I was feeling more than just woozy. It was as if the air was thick, making it hard to catch my breath. But I seemed to be the only one with this problem. I looked at my watch and saw it was almost six, so I figured

I could sneak out early and head home. Normally, I would not have left until seven.

As I walked to the parking lot, the cool December air felt good on my face, but I still had trouble breathing. When I finally got to my car, I called my husband to let him know I was on my way home.

I tried to be casual as I mentioned having trouble catching my breath. I told him that it felt like I was having an allergic reaction to something, except for the minor detail that I didn't have any allergies.

When I got home, I ate dinner, put the kids to bed, showered, worked, and went to sleep.

When I woke up in the morning, I felt a little better, but the heaviness in my chest hadn't completely subsided.

The next day, during a business lunch, I felt like food was getting caught in my throat. I tried to act casual, but I was concerned and very distracted.

By the end of the day, my throat felt tight and my breathing felt constricted again. This pattern continued for several days.

About a week later, I was scheduled for an executive physical. This was a great perk of the job, where I was entitled to a complete medical workup at UCLA with their top physicians.

I met with the doctor in his office when all the tests were finished. He was happy to congratulate me on my outstanding health and marveled that I was a forty-year-old woman who had just given birth to my third child. He asked me if I had any questions or concerns.

I must admit, I was a bit taken aback. I was sure that he was going to say he'd found something wrong with my throat or thyroid. Or, at the very least, something peculiar in my lungs.

I was completely confused by my clean bill of health.

I casually said, "Yeah, I just have one question. I have trouble taking deep breaths, and I feel like something is caught in my throat."

The doctor looked puzzled and scanned the test results again.

He said, "I can assure you there is nothing in your throat, but what do you mean you can't catch your breath? Does this happen all the time?"

I said, "It's been since I returned to work after my maternity leave."

He asked, "Do you exercise?"

"I play tennis on the weekends."

"How long do you play?"

"On average, about two to three hours, if I have someone to watch my kids."

He frowned. "You don't have any problems breathing when you play tennis?"

"No."

"Have you had any big changes in your life recently?"

"Well, kind of. I got divorced, met someone new, got engaged, sold our respective homes, bought and remodeled a new home together, got married, and just had another baby. This is my third child, but my husband's first."

"When did all that happen?"

"Over the last eighteen months."

He waited a beat and then said, "I don't think you have a breathing problem. I think you might be suffering from anxiety."

I said, "Oh no, the changes in my personal life are all great. I've never been happier. It's my job that's stressing me out."

Back in those days, I worked like a crazy person. I would usually spend ten to twelve hours out of the house. Then, I would come home for dinner, put the kids to bed, and start working again until it was time to go to sleep. I felt like I never got a break. I even worked on Sundays.

That day in my office, when I felt like I was suffocating, what I was actually experiencing was my first panic attack.

Before that day, my operating manual had always been a recipe of the following: hypervigilance + multitasking + overthinking + people-pleasing + perfectionism.

It had all worked pretty well for forty years, but now, suddenly, my operating manual had become my kryptonite. My capacity to have it all and do it all was overheating, backfiring, and malfunctioning.

I needed a new manual, but I didn't have one.

Overthinking is a common trait for people with analytical brains. It's not a medical condition but a colloquial term for worrying about every possible outcome.

In my work as a coach, I realize that many of my clients who suffer from overthinking also exhibit tendencies of people-pleasing and perfectionism. These come together to create a holy trinity of coping mechanisms that I will discuss in more detail in the chapters ahead. But for now, let's talk about some of the notable traits of an overthinker:

- Insomnia—trouble falling asleep, staying asleep, or both

- Ruminating thoughts
- Replaying conversations in your head
- Worrying incessantly
- Catastrophizing (imagining the worst possible outcome)
- Difficulty letting go of things
- Fear of the unknown
- Self-doubt
- Analysis paralysis

Although the average human has about 60,000 thoughts a day, overthinking is different from just having thoughts. It's obsessing over a thought or thoughts, doubting your ability to make a decision, and ruminating over things longer than necessary. This pattern of behavior comes at a cost. That cost might be time, money, energy, or even your relationships.

Overthinking might look like any one of these scenarios:

- Obsessing about something that you did or didn't do
- Obsessing about something that you wish you had said or not said
- Obsessing about something that you want but don't think you deserve
- Obsessing about something that could happen but hasn't happened yet

Exhausting, right?!

When I had my first panic attack, my body was telling me to slow down. I was way over the "speed limit," and then it got to a point where my body was breaking down from the stress.

I was sleep deprived. I was worried about having the energy to handle a newborn baby. I was worried about my new babysitter taking care of my kids twelve hours a day. I was worried about my new marriage suffering from me being spread too thin. I was worried about my older kids adjusting to their stepdad. I was worried about getting enough time with my older kids as I shared custody with my ex-husband. I was worried about the volume of work I had every day. I was worried about losing my baby weight. I was worried about my new husband taking on the role of father and stepfather all at once. I was worried about my mercurial bosses. I was worried about having any time for myself.

I was worried about everything.

So how did I learn to manage my anxiety, overthinking, people-pleasing, and perfectionist brain?

I started by turning my focus inward, changing my daily habits, and learning to manage my mind.

Before my first panic attack, I was getting an A for achievement . . . but getting an F in fulfillment in the game of life.

It was time to rewrite my operating manual and learn new tools. I would love to tell you that a light switch went off and I figured it all out immediately. But no such luck. It took years of self-study, help from experts, and a lot of trial and error. So, I've compiled all those years of experience into a book so you don't have to spend twenty years trying to figure it out by yourself.

The tools I recommend in this book are intentionally simple. I want them to feel easy and uncomplicated. Some of these tools will be like telling an athlete to remember to bend their knees and watch the ball.

I heard a great story about the legendary basketball coach John Wooden. He took the UCLA team to ten national championships in his twenty-seven years as a coach. At the first practice of every season, he taught his players to put on their shoes and socks correctly. When asked why he did this, he said, "The little things matter. All I need is one little wrinkle in one sock to put a blister on one foot—and it could ruin my whole season."

The little things matter. The basics are where we start and where we return. These are the things we can control.

The tools I recommend in this book are intended to be practices. These practices will become habits over time.

During my yoga teaching certification, I learned that yogis refer to their yoga as a *practice*. No matter how long they have been practicing, teaching, or taking yoga, it is always a *practice*. The gentleness of that term has always stayed with me.

I intend for this book to be a reminder to put on your own oxygen mask first before helping others.

And with that, let's dive in . . .

CHAPTER 2

Self-Care Is Key

I f you have made it to chapter 2, then one of two things must be true:

A) We know each other, so you feel obligated to read at least one more chapter.

or

B) Something about overthinking, people-pleasing, perfectionism, or general anxiety has resonated with you.

If you fall into option A, know that I appreciate you.
If you fall into option B, know you're in the right place.

I have dealt with a low-level feeling of anxiety throughout my life. This feeling is likely due to my tendency to overthink, strive for excellence, or worry excessively. When I was a child, my dream was to become a doctor, so

I pursued a biology major on the pre-med track. However, as you may know, universities design their general education courses to weed out the weaker students.

It's fair to say that those courses (biology, chemistry, organic chemistry, physics, and calculus) decimated my self-confidence with a metaphoric weed whacker. Despite my best efforts, no amount of studying, note-taking, or determination could make up for the fact that my slightly-above-average GPA would not qualify me for admission to a prestigious medical school.

At the end of my junior year, I switched majors from biology to psychology. I considered attending law school, like my father and brother, but that wasn't for me. I also considered getting a graduate degree in psychology, but after giving up on medical school, graduate school lost its appeal.

During my senior year of college, I took a variety of electives, including television writing and a TV production course. I also did an internship at a movie studio and worked as a production assistant on a feature film. My analytical and organizational skills served me well in the frenetic world of entertainment.

When I landed my first secretarial job with a producer upon graduation, I was relieved to be on a new career track.

I imagined starting a career in the entertainment industry would be fun and a welcome departure from the academic rigor I was accustomed to. But going into the entertainment industry was not so much fun—it was more like joining the circus.

They say getting your foot in the door is the most critical step. But they fail to tell you that once your foot is in the door, it's a daily battle to hang on to the ladder, much less climb it. (Apologies for mixing my metaphors.)

Being an assistant, or secretary as they called it back then, is not glamorous work. It usually involves getting coffee, scheduling appointments, taking lunch orders, and walking your boss's dog.

There's an old joke about a guy who joins the circus and is in charge of cleaning up the elephant poop. When he complains to his friend about the menial work, his friend says, "Why don't you quit?" And the guy says, "*What?* And give up show business?"

So, once I was *in* it, I felt I had to be the best *at* it, even if that meant just getting the lunch orders right.

In the entertainment industry, there is always a risk of getting stuck on a rung or falling off the proverbial ladder. It is important to "get off the desk" before you get pigeonholed. It's about learning to identify talent—writers, actors, directors, and good material. It's also about being willing to work harder than everyone else.

Every weekend, I would take home a stack of scripts and read as many as possible. When other twenty-two-year-olds were spending their weekends going to bars, the beach, or BBQs, I was buried in script reading and watching director reels.

I cannot say I loved it as much as I wanted to succeed in it. I assumed that if I paid my dues, something good would happen, and it would all be worth it.

At the age of twenty-five, I secured my first executive position at ABC Network due to my hard work. But once again, I quickly realized that being a junior executive was just another low rung on a new ladder.

My first office at ABC had no windows and fluorescent lighting that burned my eyes, making it impossible to read scripts in my office. My wooden desk was so old and beaten up that I often snagged my stockings on the splinters. And if that wasn't fun enough, I was across from the only bathrooms on the fifth floor, so I had the pleasure of hearing flushing toilets all day.

But despite my depressing office and the fact that I was grossly underpaid relative to my male counterparts, I loved ABC because I learned a lot. I received a few promotions, was given more responsibility, and eventually got my own window office! However, I was too impatient to wait for a more coveted role and a proper salary increase, so I left after three years.

I bounced around for the next few years of my executive career, ultimately taking a job at the USA Network, where I stayed for seventeen years until I retired from my television career.

I made the mistake of assuming that things would get easier as I moved up the ranks. With every step up, I earned a bit more money, a few new titles, a staff of executives, and eventually a top creative position, a generous salary, and a corner office.

However, the politics grew exponentially with my responsibilities—and so did my anxiety.

The demands of managing a heavy workload, raising three children, handling unpredictable bosses, and the pressure to constantly churn out new hit series became overwhelming.

I was like Lucy in the candy factory. Do you remember the episode of *I Love Lucy* when Lucy and Ethel go to work in the chocolate factory? Their assignment is to take one piece of chocolate at a time and put it in the candy box. Easy-peasy. They do a great job at first and are very pleased with themselves. Until their boss turns up the speed of the conveyor belt, and the chocolates start coming so fast that they can't keep up. They end up putting them in their bras, stuffing them in their mouths, and several pieces drop on the floor.

This is how I felt most days in the television business. You work with something you love until the volume becomes too much, and your boss starts screaming at you.

I often felt unable to catch my breath during my long commutes. My neck was so stiff that I couldn't always turn my head. I suffered from stomachaches, which the doctor thought were ulcers. I had chronic headaches like clockwork every afternoon. It would take me hours to fall asleep at night.

Admittedly, I could have done a better job of self-care. But I was overstimulated, overcaffeinated, and too much of a workaholic to figure out how to slow down and manage my stress.

I loved certain aspects of my career—the prestige, the steady paycheck, and the variety of people I was working with—but I always felt like I was surviving my life instead of enjoying it.

My husband would often quip, "Your job is going to kill you." So, we started crafting an exit strategy—saving money and scaling back where possible, hoping to cash in for a more balanced life. And eventually, we did just that. However, when I finally decided to retire from the television business, my world went from overstimulated to uncomfortably quiet.

As someone who loves to be busy and productive, I had to learn to generate those qualities without a corporate structure to create them for me. It was a shock to my system, and oddly, it was very lonely at first.

While I never missed the commutes, the long days and nights, the high heels, the politics, the bureaucracy, or working every weekend and every vacation, I missed the camaraderie of my friends and the sense of purpose every day.

I realized that I felt almost the same amount of stress when I was *not* working as when I was spread too thin and overworking.

This is when I realized that being "too" busy is also a coping mechanism. Staying busy can help ward off boredom, but it may also mask feelings of inadequacy or self-doubt.

In my case, if I was busy and stressed, I could almost justify my physical and emotional pain.

But once I was no longer juggling a million balls, I had no justification for my headaches, stomachaches, and chronic muscle tension. If there was no external stress coming from my corporate life, then I couldn't justify my anxiety either. It had all become a habit . . . even my stress.

I thought retiring from my all-consuming job would resolve my anxiety issues, but when it didn't, I had to look inward. I needed to figure out how to manage my mind and body. This is why I spent a gap year blogging, getting my yoga certification to teach, practicing meditation, continuing to play tennis, and ultimately becoming a life coach.

When I discovered life coaching, I learned a lot about my overthinking brain, my people-pleasing nature, and my perfectionism, along with some fantastic tools to manage my anxiety.

Which leads me to some good news and some bad news.

The bad news is there is no magic bullet.

The good news is that this book is packed with many of the incredible tools I learned. Some you will like and some you won't. Use the ones that resonate with you and leave the rest.

The first key to reducing stress and anxiety is *self-care*.

And no, I'm not talking about massages, facials, or spa days, although those are nice too. I'm talking about *daily* self-care—a routine, a checklist, a guide that helps you maintain a greater sense of calm and confidence.

Overthinkers tend to worry a lot. We spend a lot of unnecessary energy overanalyzing, overworrying, and over-doing. As I mentioned before, overthinking often manifests with other traits like people-pleasing and perfectionism.

So why are these tendencies a problem? Well, they aren't, in small doses. The problem is when these traits become habitual and unmanaged, leading to burnout and resentment.

When you find yourself saying things like . . .

"No one else cares as much as I do."

"No one else listens the way I do."

"No one else does it like I do."

"No one will get things done if I don't do it myself."

If this sounds like you, then you're probably very busy taking care of everyone and everything.

When I was raising my children, working in a corporate job sixty to seventy hours a week, trying to maintain a marriage and meet the obligations of friends and extended family, I put myself on the back burner.

I had no self-care routine and didn't prioritize my health. I only knew how to react to my physical symptoms, which was like playing Whac-A-Mole with my stress-related ailments. I ran from doctor to doctor and practitioner to practitioner, trying to put the stuffing back in the proverbial scarecrow. I was not thinking holistically or connecting my mind to my body. Like many others, I was just like a chicken running around without its head.

During my gap year of self-discovery, self-care, and learning to connect my mind to my body, I devised a daily checklist for what I refer to as the non-negotiables. These are the most foundational aspects of my coaching practice and lifestyle.

I call the checklist HOME (or HOME *work* for task-oriented people). Each letter of HOME represents one of the four pillars of my daily self-care routine.

H = Hydration
O = Observe Your Levels
M = Meditation
E = Exercise

Welcome HOME! Are you ready to get started?

CHAPTER 3

Hydration

H *is for Hydration.*
    If you already drink a minimum of 64 ounces of water daily, congratulations! You're welcome to skip ahead to the next chapter.

An adult human is composed of approximately 60 percent water. Water is crucial in ensuring that every aspect of our body functions properly.

Fun fact: Dehydration can mimic anxiety and depression.

Dehydration can have a stressful impact on your body. It can cause a drop in blood pressure and an increase in heart rate. It can lead to dizziness and is often mistaken for anxiety. Moreover, dehydration can harm the production of serotonin, a neurotransmitter responsible for mood. When there is a lack of serotonin, you may experience feelings of depression or a decline in your energy level. But there are so many other physical reasons to stay hydrated.

TEMPERATURE REGULATION

The body dissipates heat through sweat—a critical function for preventing overheating during physical activity or exposure to high temperatures. Dehydration compromises this mechanism, increasing the risk of illnesses such as heat exhaustion and heatstroke.

In other words, just like a car, you're prone to overheating if you aren't watching your temperature gauge. But since we don't come with gauges, we must be mindful of water intake, especially in hot climates or while exercising.

CARDIOVASCULAR HEALTH

The circulatory system relies on adequate fluid levels to maintain blood volume and pressure. Dehydration can decrease blood flow, increasing the strain on the heart and potentially elevating blood pressure.

JOINT LUBRICATION AND CUSHIONING

The synovial fluid surrounding joints relies on hydration for proper viscosity, ensuring smooth movement and reducing friction between bones. Inadequate hydration can contribute to joint stiffness and discomfort.

Whether you're an older person or an athlete, you know how painful it can be when your joints are achy. Water plays an essential role in reducing pain and keeping things moving.

COGNITIVE FUNCTION

Dehydration has been shown to impair concentration, memory, and overall cognitive performance. The brain depends on a delicate balance of water and electrolytes for optimal signaling between neurons. Even mild dehydration can result in noticeable cognitive deficits.

In basic terms, water can help you think better!

ATHLETIC PERFORMANCE AND RECOVERY

During physical activity, the body loses water through sweating, and it is vital to maintain fluid balance to avoid dehydration. Dehydration can cause increased fatigue, decreased endurance, and a higher risk of muscle cramps. Water is crucial for athletic success.

RADIANT SKIN

Proper hydration is shown to improve skin elasticity, flush out toxins, and help fight acne.

BETTER ORGAN FUNCTION

Staying hydrated can reduce the risk of kidney stones, especially for those who consume a lot of caffeine.

WEIGHT MANAGEMENT

Drinking water can be a key player in a successful weight loss program. Many people mistake dehydration for hunger. Drinking water can help you feel fuller longer. It's a better alternative to high-calorie drinks, such as shakes, juices, sodas, and sugary coffee drinks.

IMMUNE SUPPORT

Drinking plenty of water can help flush bacteria and toxins out of your body, keeping you healthier during cold and flu season.

BETTER DIGESTION

Constipation is often a lack of water in the bowels. Hydration helps keep things moving.

HEADACHE PREVENTION

Dehydration is one of the leading causes of headaches. Staying hydrated can help prevent headaches and reduce reliance on medication.

BETTER BREATH

Dehydration can lead to halitosis, which is a medical condition commonly known as bad breath. Of course, water is not a substitute for good dental hygiene, but it can be a breath saver.

If you're inconsistent about your water intake, try getting yourself a cup you love or a water bottle you like carrying.

Sometimes, increasing our water intake is about making it more appealing. Another trick is to add a little squeeze of fresh lemon, lime, or orange to your water. Some people add cucumber or mint.

The only thing I don't recommend is adding anything artificial. I don't advocate buying or adding artificial sweetener drops, packages, or flavorings.

So grab a glass of water and move on to the next letter in HOME.

CHAPTER 4

Observe Your Levels

Welcome to the Big O.

Well, wait—this might not be what you think.

The O in HOME means Observe Your Levels.

As we discussed in the previous chapter on hydration, it's easy to mistake dehydration for other sensations, such as low energy, depression, anxiety, headaches, and even hunger. That's why I always recommend checking your hydration levels first. However, if you're sufficiently hydrated and still experiencing any of those symptoms, it's time to go down the rest of the checklist.

Observing your levels has a two-part question:

Do I need to eat, or do I need to rest?

I run on pretty high energy. I rarely drink caffeine, and I eat very little refined sugar. However, I have low blood sugar, so when my blood sugar levels start dropping, I can suddenly become quiet, irritable, and tired.

When I was younger, my idea of breakfast was to grab a cup of coffee with a pastry or a bagel. I would eat a sandwich, pizza, pasta, or something with heavy carbs for lunch. I would feel full for about an hour and then be exhausted. This resulted in me consuming more caffeine or snacking on sugary or carbohydrate-rich foods all afternoon.

As I got older, I realized that I was living in a cycle of spiking my blood sugar and then crashing. When I felt the crash, I would refuel with more sugar or caffeine. The sugar might have been more carbohydrates, like a leftover pastry or pretzels, or it might have been literal sugar, like candy or an afternoon soda.

In my corporate life, Coca-Cola was my drug of choice every afternoon around 3:00 p.m. when I would start to crash.

By the time I got home at 7:00 p.m., I was so ravenous, exhausted, and cranky that I would eat anything in front of me. So, between the cortisol and adrenaline that I was creating all day in my stressful job, I was making things worse with a high-carb diet and self-medicating with excess sugar and caffeine.

I was utterly taxing out my adrenal glands.

No wonder I had difficulty falling asleep at night and getting up in the morning.

I later came to realize that I needed to eat some kind of protein at every meal and plan a protein-rich snack in the afternoon. Protein sources might be different for everyone depending on your dietary restrictions.

- If you're an omnivore (someone who eats everything), then protein might be beef, pork, veal, chicken, turkey, fish, shellfish, eggs, dairy products, nuts, nut butters, tofu, legumes, seeds, or beans.

- If you're a pescatarian, your protein choices might include fish, seafood, legumes, beans, tofu, dairy products, nuts, nut butters, and seeds.
- If you're a vegetarian, this might include dairy, eggs, tofu, legumes, beans, nuts, nut butters, and seeds.
- If you're a vegan, it might mean tofu, legumes, beans, nuts, nut butters, and seeds only.

But the point is, if you feel yourself getting lethargic, cranky, or having trouble concentrating, you must ask yourself: "Do I need to eat a meal or a healthy snack?"

Planning your meals, or at least having a go-to healthy snack, can prevent the crash or feeling hangry.

Protein stabilizes blood sugar and keeps you full longer. So, whether you're trying to build muscle, lose weight, or stay more focused, protein is your friend. Protein is the building block of our muscles and our brain function.

People always ask what healthy protein they can eat in the afternoon as a quick snack.

Here's a list:

- Natural peanut butter or other nut butters
- Nuts or seeds
- Hard-boiled eggs
- Turkey slices (no additives)
- Protein bars (no additives)
- Protein shakes (no additives)

- Greek yogurt (if no dairy sensitivities)
- Cheese (if no dairy sensitivities)

Any of these proteins can be paired with cut-up vege-tables or a piece of fresh fruit for a more satisfying snack.

The trick is to read labels! If you eat snacks that come in a package, you need to be able to pronounce the ingredients on the label. This is especially true for protein bars, pro-tein powders, and the like. Ideally, avoid high fructose corn syrup, refined sugar, and especially artificial sweeteners.

Artificial sweeteners are often marketed as a healthy substitute for sugar, as they do not contain calories. How-ever, these sweeteners are chemicals that trick the brain into believing it is consuming something sweet. Some studies have shown that when the body does not receive the sugar it was promised, it can lead us to crave more sugar or calories.

During my college days, diet sodas and frozen yogurt were the most popular choices among weight-conscious people. I, too, was a big fan of both. However, by the time I graduated, I had gained twenty pounds. It wasn't just the typical first-year fifteen that many students experience in college. The problem was that I had consumed too many chemicals and artificial sweeteners, which left me feeling hungry all the time, and craving more food—especially carbs.

Many believe that artificial sweeteners can help in weight loss, but the truth is that they may lead to weight gain for many people.

If you have a sweet tooth, it's better to opt for natural sources of sweetness. Fresh fruits make an excellent dessert choice, and you can also use small amounts of pure maple syrup or honey instead of refined sugar to sweeten things up. Additionally, dark chocolate can be a great little treat, but remember to consume it in moderation.

Of course, no one says you must avoid desserts for the rest of your life. I'm talking about daily eating habits to maintain optimal health and energy and to reduce feelings of anxiety or depression.

Eating a well-balanced diet is only part of a healthy lifestyle. Still, it is not a substitute for seeking professional help if you're diagnosed with clinical depression, anxiety, or other mental health issues.

So, "Do I need to eat?" is the first part of observing your levels.

Now for part two.

If you know you're well-hydrated and well-fed but you're still tired, you need to take a break and rest. If you generally experience fatigue sometime between lunch and dinner during the workweek, you have a few options.

- If you have an office or work from home, lie down for a five- or ten-minute break.
- If you're in a cubicle, close your eyes at your desk for a few minutes.
- If neither is available, take a power nap in a breakroom.

In my previous executive role, I used to take a short break after lunch in my parked car to rest my eyes and brain before heading back to the office. Another option when feeling tired is to get fresh air or walk around the block.

If afternoon fatigue is a chronic issue for you and you have changed your diet, you might want to examine your sleep hygiene at night: Do you have a bedtime routine? Or are you up late watching TV, scrolling on social media, or playing video games?

Do you have trouble falling asleep or staying asleep due to overthinking, chronic or acute pain, or indigestion?

Some people are fortunate enough to fall asleep easily, while others struggle with it. The men in my family are all blessed with the gift of easy sleep. Unfortunately, the women didn't inherit that gene. I used to have trouble both falling and staying asleep until I improved my sleep hygiene. It's still not perfect, but it's so much better than it was.

Here are some of the typical culprits of sleep issues.

CAFFEINE

Coffee, tea, some sodas, kombucha, and energy drinks all contain caffeine. If sleep is an issue for you, then I recommend limiting your caffeine to one cup a day and not after 2:00 p.m.

ALCOHOL

While alcohol can help people relax and even fall asleep, it can be a sleep disruptor, as your liver has to process that foreign substance. According to Chinese medicine, the liver cleansing cycle is between 2:00 and 5:00 a.m., which is why so many people wake up during those hours. Skipping alcohol can be critical to a better night's sleep.

FOOD

A classic sleep disruptor is overeating or eating too late. Another is sugar intake.

Watching what you eat in the evenings and eliminating these stimulants can help you get a good night's rest.

Then there's practicing a good bedtime routine. Here is a checklist for that.

- Set a bedtime.
- Turn off all electronic devices an hour before bed.
- Read a book, write in a journal, or meditate before bed to relax your nervous system.
- Keep your room cool.
- If you experience anxiety, consider using a weighted blanket.
- Cover all LED lights in the room (TV, DVR, alarm clocks, power strips, computers, etc.).
- If you're bothered by noise, try using earplugs.
- If light is a problem, use a weighted eye mask.

Most people require seven to eight hours of sleep per night, although this may vary. But even if you get a good night's sleep, there is nothing wrong with a power nap or rest in the afternoon if your job or schedule permits it.

You might be wondering how this all relates to overthinking.

Hunger and exhaustion can create feelings of anxiety. When our bodies are not performing optimally, our brains can spin out, *looking for* problems. It's a form of *negativity* or *confirmation bias*—when something has gone wrong (physically, mentally, or emotionally), we start looking for more evidence that things are going wrong. So when our bodies are not feeling well, we might start thinking about that friend who didn't respond to our last text. Or we worry that we will get fired for missing a deadline. Or we wonder if our partner is still attracted to us since we can't remember the last time they complimented us. In other words, we're looking to confirm the reasons that we're feeling anxious or depressed.

It doesn't take much for our brains to start down this rabbit hole. However, we can create a greater sense of calm by learning to manage our minds and by listening to our bodies. I cannot tell you how many times I thought the world was ending, and then I took a quick nap or ate a snack, and suddenly, everything was right with the world again.

Try observing your levels next time you feel like you're starting to spin out by asking yourself this simple question: Do I need to rest, or do I need a healthy snack?

And now let's move on to the next letter of HOME . . .

CHAPTER 5

Meditation

All right, we are halfway HOME.
M is for Meditation.

Once again, if meditation is already part of your daily practice, you can skip this chapter and move to the next one.

I admit that this pillar of HOME can be the most challenging. I know it was for me.

As a consummate overthinker, people-pleaser, and perfectionist, I contemplated and worried about everything. I struggled to manage my overthinking brain. A friend told me I needed to learn to meditate, but I had a million reasons not to.

My biggest excuse for not meditating was that I didn't have time.

There's a popular expression in the meditation community: If you don't have time to meditate for ten minutes, then you probably need to meditate for twenty.

But time wasn't my only excuse. I had a list of others:

- "I tried it, but it doesn't work for me."
- "I cannot sit still with my eyes closed."
- "Meditation makes me *more* anxious."
- "I don't have a quiet place to meditate without being disturbed."

Most of us don't want to meditate because we don't want to be alone with our thoughts. Closing our eyes without the intention of going to sleep can feel a little scary. Sitting alone in silence can feel tedious, unproductive, and oddly overwhelming.

This is more true than ever in a world addicted to constant stimulation. Our smartphones are like having the entire world in our pocket—texts, voicemails, calendars, social media, music, entertainment, and the potential to connect to 7.9 billion other people! No wonder we don't want to close our eyes and be alone with our thoughts for a few minutes.

I was determined to overcome my reluctance to sit alone quietly every day. So, I enrolled in a Transcendental Meditation (TM) course. During the first session, I felt like I would crawl out of my skin when I had to sit for twenty minutes in silence with my eyes closed. I felt that root canals were less irritating than learning to meditate.

TM involves sitting silently for twenty minutes twice daily, using a one-word mantra. Initially, I had difficulty sitting still and felt restless and uncomfortable. However, with practice, I learned to meditate, and I came to appreciate the discipline, serenity, and tranquility it brings. I enjoyed it so much that I even taught my dog to lie beside me during my morning meditation sessions, and now we both look forward to it.

Once I got the hang of it, I couldn't wait to share the gift of meditation with my family and friends. Meditation taught me how to observe my thoughts without constantly reacting to them. It has made me calmer, more centered, and more creative.

But despite my enthusiasm, very few of my friends and family members were eager to embark on such a disciplined practice.

During the pandemic, I believed sharing meditation with those experiencing anxiety was more important than ever. But I needed to find a way to make it more accessible than TM, which was too much of a barrier to entry for most folks. This is when I discovered guided meditation.

There are many kinds of meditation: mindful (breath and focus), transcendental (one-word mantra), guided (someone narrating a message), loving-kindness (mantra or phrase), yoga (postures and breath work), body scan (focusing on one body part at a time), spiritual, Zen (specific posture and breathing), chakra (focusing on energy centers), and even walking meditations.

Guided meditation opened a whole new world for me, and that's when I decided I could teach anyone to meditate. I recorded my five- and ten-minute meditations and uploaded them to my YouTube channel. Since then, thousands of people have enjoyed listening to them for free.

Strangers have sent me notes thanking me for providing them with comfort and peace. It feels so good that I can reach people worldwide and bring a few minutes of peace to their day.

Meditation is truly the secret sauce for learning to sit with your thoughts and detach from them. It has given me the courage to start a second career as a life coach and the confidence and vision to start blogging, podcasting, and writing this book.

Meditation has been instrumental in my own healing process from various sports injuries and stress-related aches and pains. Although meditation can have spiritual aspects, it's not tied to any specific religion. Therefore, anyone can practice it, regardless of faith or agnostic beliefs. Meditation provides an opportunity to connect with a powerful force within oneself.

Our brains are the most incredible encyclopedias, supercomputers, pharmacies, resources, and connections to the rest of the universe. When you tap into the serenity of your mind and connect it to your body, you're unstoppable! You learn to harness the power of your talent and well-being. Learning to sit quietly with your thoughts is the ultimate power and source of inspiration.

The most significant error people make while learning to meditate is assuming they must be perfect. We are so conditioned to think that we must look like something we've seen on television, in the movies, or on social media.

One client told me she couldn't start meditating until her meditation cushion arrived.

Another client said he couldn't meditate because he was never alone in his home.

And another told me they couldn't sit still for ten minutes without fidgeting. (By the way, this is true for most beginners.)

Here's the key to meditation: let go of perfection!

Keep in mind:

- There's no perfect chair or cushion.
- It will rarely be silent.
- People who don't meditate might judge you.
- You might be uncomfortable at first.
- You might think you need the right music, incense, or treehouse in Bali to do it right.

None of that is true.

Find a comfortable spot, close your eyes, or look downward, to minimize distractions. Put on your headphones and listen to a guided meditation on YouTube or a meditation app. Start with five minutes and build up to as long as needed. If you're interrupted, it's okay. Just keep going.

I recommend meditating first thing in the morning because it starts your day from a place of grounded energy. Schedule it until it becomes a habit, like brushing your teeth—you wouldn't think of leaving the house without doing it first.

One of my favorite things to do before meditation is to set an intention for the day. It can be anything you want it to be. Here are some examples. My intention for the day is:

- to be grateful
- to heal
- to help someone
- to be grounded
- to be confident
- to be stronger

- to be brave
- to be creative
- to be productive

Your intention can be as specific or as general as you want. Setting an intention supercharges your meditation and sets you up for better success in your day.

Just as rocket fuel empowers a rocket to break free from Earth's gravitational pull, setting daily intentions and meditation help individuals transcend the mind's constraints and find a higher consciousness.

And with that, let's blast off to the final pillar of HOME.

CHAPTER 6

Exercise

The last letter of HOME is E.
E is for Exercise.

Now, if you already love to work out, play a sport, or have an exercise routine, move to the head of the class and skip to the next chapter. But for those who don't have a regular exercise routine, keep reading.

Regular exercise is a powerful tool for boosting self-esteem. It improves physical appearance and profoundly affects mental well-being by silencing our inner over-thinker, people-pleaser, and perfectionist. Exercise also boosts endorphins, serotonin, and dopamine levels, the neurochemicals associated with happiness and pleasure.

Exercise keeps you in good shape, burns calories, maintains muscle tone, and makes you feel younger and more energetic. Additionally, it can be a great way to meet people.

Whether you go to a gym, take walks with a friend, run marathons or triathlons, or play sports like tennis, pickleball, or golf, you're engaged with other people. So exercise can be a great way to create or maintain a social life.

When I was in my late thirties, I had two little kids and a full-time job as a television executive.

Which meant I had zero *me time*.

My former assistant noticed that I was experiencing chronic stress and recommended that I take up a hobby. At the time, I didn't understand what she meant because I had never played a sport before, and I couldn't recall ever having a hobby.

Before having children, I would go to the gym a few days a week. I would sit on the stationary bike or climb the StairMaster with a script in hand. I don't think any sweating was involved, but I felt like I was killing two birds with one stone. Multitasking was my jam. But once I had kids, my gym routine went by the wayside.

I told my assistant that I didn't have time for a hobby. She insisted that I create time. You might say that she was my first life coach. She provided me with a list of potential hobbies, including taking Spanish, tennis, or pottery.

I chose tennis and found a coach to hit with me for thirty minutes every Saturday morning. Although I enjoyed it, I was not very good at it. I would hit the ball as hard as possible without learning any actual techniques like serving or volleying or even keeping score. I realized I needed to meet other tennis players to improve my game, so I joined a tennis club. After playing for about eighteen months, I was still only at a beginner's level. One Sunday morning, I asked a guy I had briefly met to hit with me. The conversation went like this:

Me (friendly): "Do you want to hit?"

The guy (confused): "With you?"

Me (a bit defensive): "Uh, yeah."

The guy (reluctant): "I guess."

At the time, I failed to appreciate that the guy I'd asked to hit with me was the club champion and I was an absolute beginner. I was so naive about the game that I didn't realize there were different levels of play. And yet, he pulled his racket out of his tennis bag, and we hit for a few minutes. We were bumped off the court after not realizing a tournament was scheduled for that afternoon. As we were vacating the court, our dialogue continued:

The guy: "You're not as bad as you look."

Me (a bit put off but trying to play it cool): "Thanks?!"

That might have been my last interaction with him had he not been such a good player and so attractive. But there was chemistry between us, and soon we found ourselves arranging mixed-doubles games and grabbing a bite to eat after the matches. Within a few weeks, we started dating.

A year later, we were married.

Tennis was my very first sport, and it provided a window into a whole new social life, romantic life, and commitment to exercise. I have been playing tennis for over twenty years now, and my husband (the guy from the tennis club) and I have been together ever since.

I'm not suggesting that taking up a sport will change the entire trajectory of your personal life. In my case, taking up tennis was a way to create a hobby and a distraction from my demanding work life. But it had many unforeseen benefits—new friends, a new life partner, and a great way to stay in shape.

Although I wish that I could play tennis every day, it is too hard on body. But I still ensure that I engage in some form of movement for at least twenty minutes daily. It might be pickleball, yoga, spinning, walking, or stretching.

You don't have to play a sport to be active. You just need to move. You can exercise in front of your television. You can dance in your basement. You can hula-hoop with your kids. You can take daily walks with your dog.

Consistency is key in the HOME model, just like in everything else. Your daily habits play a vital role in achieving your other goals. While having a workout buddy or someone to exercise with can be more enjoyable, it's okay to do it alone. The secret is to find something you love doing. If you love it, you're more likely to stick with it.

If you have trouble staying motivated, then find an accountability partner. Your accountability partner might be your spouse, roommate, best friend, coworker, family member, or neighbor. You can also hire a personal trainer or join a gym and find someone to be your workout buddy. By having to commit to someone else, you're less likely to cancel or come up with an excuse.

The other trick to being consistent is to schedule your exercise. Make it an appointment on your calendar!

If you're a morning person, exercise in the morning. If you're more of a night owl, try exercising before dinner.

If you don't have time before or after work, take a walk or go to the gym during lunch.

Regular exercise is crucial for managing stress, anxiety, depression, and improving your self-image.

HOME is a checklist for creating a daily routine, but it is also a way to manage your mind-body connection. I use it every day as part of my self-regulation.

Many of us tend to misjudge our biochemistry and assume that we're feeling anxious or depressed. But often, we don't listen to what our bodies need throughout the day.

If you take time to do your HOME work every day, you will feel less anxious, more energetic, and more grounded. An exercise routine can boost your confidence, creativity, and joy, transforming you from a Burned-Out Betty to a Motivated Mindy.

Now that you have your HOME work, are you ready for additional tools to help manage your overthinking brain?

CHAPTER 7

Spinning

A former colleague and dear friend introduced me to spinning.

I'm not talking about stationary bikes or dancing in circles. I'm talking about when your thoughts take you down a rabbit hole of worry, negativity, and obsessive thinking, aka overthinking.

We tend to be most vulnerable to spinning when lying down at night because we are physically and emotionally exhausted. For some of us, it might be our first time alone with our thoughts all day.

My friend used to say, "It's important to recognize when your sleep train arrives and to get on board because, otherwise, you might miss your train and keep spinning."

But if you struggle to fall asleep, I want to offer some tricks to help you access your sleep train and stop the "spins."

In a previous chapter, I talked about the importance of good sleep hygiene. However, I understand that some people may still have trouble turning off those thoughts, even if they practice good sleep habits.

Remember those 60,000 thoughts we have per day? Well, 90 percent of those thoughts are repetitive, and that can create the spins or negative thought spirals.

Journaling is an effective way to escape negative thought spirals. Grab a notebook or a notepad and start journaling before bed to get those annoying thoughts out of your head.

There are many misconceptions about journaling, similar to those associated with meditation.

You don't need to have the perfect journal or notebook.

If you're waiting for some fancy Italian leather-bound, gold-embossed, handmade, monogrammed work of art until you start journaling, let that go.

You don't need to have the perfect writing instrument.

We have all seen too many movies about the tortured writer or philosopher who sits down at a mahogany desk in their study, writing their memoirs with a fancy pen and inkwell. Let that go, too.

You don't need to have perfect spelling or grammar.

It doesn't matter if you're an English major or even formally educated; no one is reading this, and no one is grading it.

Journaling has no rules.

You can write your thoughts on paper, in a binder, in a diary, on your phone, or on your computer. You can write with a pen, pencil, crayon, or keyboard. Just write. Don't edit. You can always edit later if you want to.

The most common mistake in journaling is letting the perfectionist get in the way.

Journaling is just like taking out the garbage. It's a

decluttering mechanism. It is a practice to help process your thoughts and not let them fester. Think of your ruminating thoughts like stagnant water. They can grow bacteria or fungi, which become unhealthy and stinky. When water is allowed to move, it stays fresh. Your mind is no different from that container of water.

Let the water flow and let the thoughts go.

By journaling before bedtime, you can usher those nagging thoughts, bothersome conversations, and hurt feelings out of your head and onto your paper or computer. Then you can rest.

Journaling can be a powerful tool for starting your day too! While you're less likely to have those spinning thoughts first thing in the morning, journaling can help set an intention for your day and meditation practice. It can also be beneficial any time of the day that you have ruminating thoughts that are getting in your way.

If you hate to write or type, then try recording your thoughts. Most smartphones will record your voice. The objective is to have a safe space to get annoying thoughts out of your head.

Once again, there are no rules.

You don't have to write or speak for any specific time.

You don't have to share your words or thoughts with anyone.

You don't have to be rational.

You don't have to edit.

You just let it rip.

And then something magical happens. You will likely feel less burdened, anxious, and annoyed. If you aren't sure where to start, you can use writing prompts like these:

- I feel . . .
- Today I was . . .
- I am . . .
- I would like . . .
- I wish . . .
- Today I learned . . .
- I feel anxious about . . .
- I'm grateful for . . .

I have kept journals off and on throughout my life. Now, I have numerous boxes filled with my journals. Occasionally, I go back and read them, and I'm amazed by the small things that used to bother me. The most exciting part is realizing that the things that used to stress me out are no longer a concern today.

Journaling has many benefits, like reminding us that everything is temporary, including situations, thoughts, and emotions, which come and go. (I will explore this concept more in depth in a later chapter.) When I look back at my journals, I feel grateful for having navigated, survived, and overcome whatever challenges I faced at the time.

When I was nearing the end of my TV career, I began writing a weekly blog. That blog helped me develop the skills to start a second blog when I became a coach. Those blogs gave birth to my podcast, *The Overthinker's Guide to Joy*, which helped me create the foundation for this book.

Journaling is a powerful tool to manage your mind, providing a release valve from the pressure in your head and heart, even if you're not interested in writing or podcasting.

But what if you have good sleep hygiene and journal

before bed but *still* have trouble falling asleep? Or perhaps you wake up in the middle of the night and can't fall back asleep? I have a few more tools for those extra-stubborn late-night spins.

Try a sleep meditation. Many apps offer guided meditations specifically for sleep. If your partner doesn't want to hear a guided meditation, try using headphones, earbuds, or a sleep mask that has Bluetooth headphones sewn into it.

When I wake up in the middle of the night, and my brain starts to dwell on a nagging thought, a work issue, or a project I'm working on, I'll use the mantra, "Not now." I'm not judging the thoughts. I'm sleep-training my brain to let go of these thoughts for the time being and fall back asleep. Our brains are like puppies; they might wake up and whine in the middle of the night, but it's our job to remind them that they're safe, but it's not time to play.

Another trick I like to do is to put one hand over my heart and one hand over my belly and focus on my breath.

If that is not enough to calm my nervous system, I will use a specific method of breathing called "box breathing." Box breathing refers to the four sides of a box, which is good to visualize while doing this exercise.

- Inhale slowly to a count of four.
- Hold for a count of four.
- Exhale slowly for a count of four.
- Hold for a count of four.

Repeat the set for a total of four times.

Navy SEALs use this technique to regulate their nervous systems in combat and when trying to fall asleep to alleviate their anxiety and frantic thoughts.

Don't strive for perfection. Instead, experiment with different options and see what works best for you.

CHAPTER 8

Three More Habits to Create Calm

Since we're halfway through the book, let's recap. Here are the tools I have recommended so far:

HOME: Hydration

                Observe Your Levels

                Meditation

                Exercise

If you're being honest, which habits do you already practice, and which ones are you ready to try or practice more consistently?

- More water, less caffeine, less alcohol?
- Better diet?
- More rest?

- More consistency in exercise?
- More consistency in meditation?
- Starting to journal?

Now, let's say you already do *all* these things, and you're still feeling anxious or blue—let's add some more tools to the toolbox.

As I have said, I believe in having a daily routine. Although many creative types think routine is the enemy of creativity, I beg to differ. Most behavioral psychologists and researchers agree that routine is a great way to manage anxiety and stress, which is how we nurture and harness creative energy. So, let's talk about three more habits.

1. ESTABLISH A GOOD MORNING ROUTINE

Using the HOME model is an excellent place to start. You want to start your morning with a big glass of water because our bodies wake up dehydrated. I have also recommended a morning meditation to set an intention for your day. If you have time to exercise before work, that is ideal too. However, so many of us hit the snooze button as long as we can, then roll out of bed, drink coffee, grab a pastry, and run out the door.

But if you can get up forty-five minutes earlier than usual, you'll have time to drink water, do a five-minute meditation, get twenty minutes of exercise, and grab a protein-based breakfast.

This new routine will not only change your brain chemistry by flooding it with endorphins and serotonin (those happy neurochemicals we talked about earlier), but it will also result in your feeling more powerful and grounded as you enter your workday.

Another great part of a morning routine is to tidy up as you go. Little things like making your bed in the morning can set you up for success.

Admiral William McRaven, a retired Navy veteran, wrote a book called *Make Your Bed*. This simple step was one of his key takeaways from a lifetime of military service. He writes, "If you make your bed every morning, you will have accomplished the first task of the day. It will give you a small sense of pride and it will encourage you to do another task and another and another. By the end of the day, that one task completed will have turned into many tasks completed."

The same goes for your kitchen. Don't leave dirty dishes in the sink. Put them in the dishwasher or wash them as you use them. Waking up to a clean kitchen can have a positive impact on your day. Tidying up is just one element of a good morning routine, but here's another trick to keeping things tidy.

2. DECLUTTER: SIMPLIFY YOUR LIFE

You don't need to go full-tilt Marie Kondo. You can start with something small like your purse. Or one closet. Or your car. Here are some basic steps to get you started:

- First, get a box of heavy-duty trash bags or boxes separated into trash, donations, and recycling. Label them clearly and make sure you have enough.

- Identify what you use and what you don't. Then, keep it, donate it, or throw it away.
- Get rid of the bags and boxes labeled trash.
- You may have to make several trips to drop off the recycling and donation bags and boxes, but don't let them pile up in your car.

One of my favorite decluttering motivators is the 27/9 feng shui (pronounced *fung shway*) challenge. You throw out or give away 27 things for 9 days in a row. The number 9 represents wealth, accomplishment, and personal goals. It also signifies heaven and earth and a sense of fullness. The number 27 represents different things in different religions and philosophies. The 2 represents balance and harmony. The 7 represents spiritual awakening and intuition. I do the 27/9 challenge several times a year because it forces me to go through old receipts, empty shoe boxes, old clothes, and even my linen closet.

The fantastic thing is that if you get rid of twenty-seven things for nine days, good things will start to happen. This might come in the form of money, new clients, opportunities, or a love interest.

The concept is that "stuff" takes energy. So, if something isn't being used or enjoyed, it weighs you down. When you're weighed down, you tend to feel more anxious or depressed.

Clearing your space, lightening your load, and tidying up will make you feel lighter. Ideally, having a place for everything or a system for things will make you more likely to follow the system daily. In other words, you will be creating an excellent new daily habit.

I have had several clients who felt they couldn't move forward in some aspect of their lives because there was too much clutter. Sometimes, they had bad spending habits because they were always buying things to "feel better."

For women, it tends to be clothing, makeup, handbags, shoes, kitchen items, or home decor. For men, it tends to be electronics, tools, toys, cars, and sports gear.

However, it can quickly become overwhelming in either case, especially when it isn't organized. The biggest problem is that people don't remember what they have and buy in duplicate. This happens a lot during grocery shopping. People tend to want to try everything or buy more than they need. They waste thousands of dollars annually by throwing out extra food or buying what they already have.

Sometimes, decluttering requires a professional. Many of my clients have hired home organizers to help them get started or do it for them. This can be very helpful in managing the overwhelm and not getting lost in the piles. When we declutter, we realize we don't need as much as we think.

We start saving money, stop wasting food, and start appreciating what we have. Once things get tidied up, it's all about consistency.

But remember, you need to let go of your perfectionism. It is not all or nothing. Like everything in this book, these are practices.

When we approach something as a practice, we exercise self-compassion while creating a new positive habit.

It's important to be mindful of how you approach your good intentions. Sometimes, we can fall into the trap of either trying too hard to make our intention perfect or doing nothing due to our fear of imperfection. This pattern of perfectionism can defeat the purpose of these habits, which are meant to bring more peace and joy into our lives. It's crucial to find a balance.

As the saying goes, "Progress, *not* perfection." Acknowledge your inner perfectionist and politely ask them to hop in the backseat. You can take the wheel from here.

If it's too overwhelming to tidy up on your own and you cannot afford to hire a professional, then consider asking a friend or relative to help you. Many people love to organize and will be happy to do so.

3. PRACTICE GRATITUDE OR JOY HUNTING

Gratitude is another practice that requires daily reps because it doesn't come naturally to most people. Our brains are wired for the opposite reaction, what I refer to as negativity bias. Here are a few examples of that trait.

Imagine purchasing a new outfit, having your hair and makeup professionally done, and feeling absolutely fantastic. People compliment you on how great you look, but then one person makes a slightly judgmental comment, and suddenly, that's all you can think about. You ignore all the positive comments and instead focus on that one negative remark.

Another example is when you ask someone for a favor, and they say no. Now you're afraid to ask someone else. You assume no one wants to help you if one person says no. You worry about being vulnerable or needy, so you do everything yourself.

Negativity bias is an antiquated survival mechanism. It was developed to alert us to danger when we were vulnerable in the wild. But we're no longer running from lions and bears. Our reptilian brains are wired to perceive danger from innocuous events like a disparaging remark or one rejection.

This issue is most evident on social media platforms.

We have become so conditioned to getting likes and positive feedback on our posts that if we receive too few likes or one negative comment, we focus only on that.

We have to retrain our brains to avoid the negativity bias trap.

We need to become *joy hunters* and *gratitude gurus*.

Becoming a joy hunter means simply being mindful of what is going right. It means focusing on the most minor details that bring you pleasure or peace.

- Relish the food or drink you consume.
- Enjoy the sunshine on your face.
- Truly listen to a compliment and allow it to soak in.
- Take the time to appreciate something in nature.
- Celebrate a piece of good news with family or friends.

Joy surrounds us, but sometimes we don't pause to let it resonate.

When I used to work in television, I often called my dad during my long commute home. While my intention was simply to say hi and catch up, I ended up venting to him about all the things that were bothering me—the heavy traffic, the high volume of work, family issues, and my challenging bosses.

He would patiently listen to me rant, and then he would lovingly remind me of his two favorite mantras: "This too shall pass" and "Count your blessings." It took me years to realize how wise his advice truly was.

When we're in pain, physically or emotionally, we tend to think that everything is permanent. But by reframing that thought to remember that everything is temporary, we can liberate ourselves from the heaviness of our situation.

"This too shall pass" has become one of my favorite meditation mantras.

As for "Count your blessings," this is the essence of joy hunting or practicing gratitude.

When we look for evidence that there is beauty in the world or positive things all around us, then we are more likely to see *more* beautiful and positive things.

When things feel dark, where can you look to count your blessings? The most obvious things tend to be what we take for granted:

- A roof over your head
- Running water
- Someone to love, even a pet
- Something to eat
- Free will

Spending a moment to count your blessings can refocus your attention on what is good and going right! This is gratitude. This is joy hunting.

And again, this is a practice.

CHAPTER 9

People-Pleasing

O verthinking is a trait, not a disorder or a diagnosis, and is often accompanied by another trait: people-pleasing.

People-pleasing is a coping mechanism and a reinforced behavior stemming from various psychological, social, and environmental factors.

Often, it is developed as a trauma response in childhood. If you had a parent or authority figure who was emotionally unstable, chances are you experienced some element of trauma as a child. It may have been the result of a parent's struggle with physical or mental health or substance abuse.

I have worked with multiple clients who had a parent who suffered from alcoholism and/or narcissism. As children, they craved the attention of that parent who was often charming and charismatic but also hurtful and neglectful. In severe cases, the dysfunctional parent was not only emotionally but also physically abusive.

I had one client whose mother was a narcissist and an alcoholic. The mother would irrationally lose her temper over the slightest thing. The father would compensate by being extra loving to his children but wouldn't address the mother's volatility or irrational behavior. The father would act like nothing was wrong. This would result in the child questioning his reality. Didn't Mom scream at us at the top of her lungs?

Didn't Mom throw a vase across the room?

The father was using codependency as a coping mechanism to deal with his irrational wife. Individuals with codependency often avoid conflict to maintain a sense of harmony and avoid potential rejection. It's another form of people-pleasing.

As a child, the messaging for my client was confusing, conflicting, and ultimately traumatizing. Like his father, he developed the coping mechanism of people-pleasing to avoid setting off his mother.

Another form of people-pleasing can manifest in becoming the perfect student or a super-high achiever in other ways, such as sports, income, or fame. In their memoirs, both Steve Martin and Matthew McConaughey wrote about their lifelong pursuit of gaining approval and connection from their fathers.

One of my clients had a father who struggled with alcoholism. When he was sober, she loved him deeply. However, when he was under the influence, he became distant and argumentative. She longed for his affection and approval, but he was often unavailable due to his alcohol addiction.

She thought that by being the perfect student and

a "good" girl, her father would see her. But to no avail. In her situation, her mother did not compensate for her father's inconsistent behavior or neglect. Her father's alcoholism left her mother feeling lonely and depressed as he was unable to connect with his family. When my client was a little girl, she believed she could comfort her mother. She became skilled at people-pleasing, hoping her mother would appreciate her love and support. Unfortunately, this was not the case. Her mother was consumed by feelings of rejection and neglect from her husband, causing her to resent her children for adding to her responsibilities.

Another client developed a habit of pleasing others due to her sibling's drug addiction. The parents were completely consumed by the sibling's problems, which included poor grades, suicidal thoughts, overdoses, and arrests. As a result, my client felt the need to compensate by becoming the good child of the family. She worked hard, achieved a 4.0 GPA, and remained quiet, organized, helpful, and perfectly polite—in other words, an ultimate people-pleaser. She carried this pattern into her adult life, striving for perfectionism in everything she did, being the pleaser in all her relationships. This left her feeling burned out and resentful at work and home.

People who always aim to please others often lose track of their own happiness and self-validation, relying solely on external approval.

Sometimes, people-pleasers want to avoid being the center of attention. They may associate too much attention with negative experiences due to their unpredictable and unreliable parents or authority figures. This can be especially true if they were raised by narcissists.

Like all of us, people-pleasers just want to be loved, valued, and acknowledged. They constantly do for others but often feel unappreciated and that no one reciprocates. This is particularly true for women, who tend to take on the traditional roles of caretaking, cooking, cleaning, and helping others. While this experience is not exclusive to women, they more readily identify as people-pleasers.

If you've been a people-pleaser for most of your life, it can become a deeply ingrained pattern of behavior. You might not even realize you're doing it half the time—it just feels like second nature. While being a people-pleaser may initially seem like a positive trait, it can ultimately be damaging. Constantly putting other people's needs ahead of your own can lead to burnout, resentment, and even a loss of self-identity.

If you bend over backward to please everyone else, perhaps you believe your needs aren't as important as everyone else's. Or you're hyper-focused on keeping the peace, even if it means sacrificing your own happiness in the process.

Depending on where you grew up, there might be strong societal norms around putting others first and avoiding confrontation at all costs. So you learn to smile and nod, even when you're screaming on the inside. But here's the thing: Beneath that smile, there can be a lot of pain and insecurity.

Maybe you don't feel like you deserve love and respect unless you constantly make others happy or prioritize their needs. Alternatively, you could be frightened by the possibility of rejection or criticism. As a result, you do everything in your power to keep everyone around you happy, even if it means disregarding your own well-being.

It's important to acknowledge the impact of trauma on one's behavior. If someone has experienced emotional or physical abuse, neglect, or any other traumatic events in the past, it can leave lasting scars that affect the way they interact with others. Sometimes, people adopt a people-pleasing personality as a coping mechanism to deal with pain and uncertainty. Seeking the approval of others allows them to feel safe.

People-pleasers are often some of the most caring and empathetic folk out there. They genuinely want to make others happy, and there's nothing wrong with that. But when it comes at the expense of their own happiness and well-being, that's when it becomes a problem.

If you constantly say yes when you want to say no, or if you're always putting others' needs before your own, it might be worth taking a step back and asking yourself why. What's driving this behavior? And more importantly, how can you break free from the cycle and develop healthier, more genuine relationships with others and yourself?

Knowing the root cause for this behavior is essential to avoid overdoing, overcommitting, people-pleasing, and connecting with what you truly want.

If feelings of burnout, resentment, and a loss of identity aren't enough to make you want to examine your people-pleasing tendencies, consider this: *People-pleasers attract narcissists.*

This is because people-pleasers seek validation by prioritizing others' needs, making them easy targets for narcissists who crave admiration and control.

In the next chapter, I will introduce you to someone who might be playing an important role in your people-pleasing persona.

CHAPTER 10

Meet Your Inner Critic

It was 1971, and I was seven years old when my mother was first diagnosed with breast cancer. She was a forty-one-year-old mother of four.

When she sat down to tell me the news, I felt like I needed to be strong for her. She told me she was going to have surgery and would be in the hospital for about two weeks. They were going to remove one of her breasts.

I was scared.

In those days, there were no phones in hospital rooms, and children under ten were not allowed to visit. The idea of her going into a hospital for two weeks without my seeing or talking to her was unimaginable to me.

Her mastectomy was brutal. Even the clinical term for her procedure was called radical, and reconstructive surgery was not an option back then. In addition to her pain, she suffered great indignity with the physical and emotional scars left behind.

She made it through the first surgery, and things looked promising. The doctors indicated that she was in remission a few months later.

But then the cancer returned to a different part of her body.

This meant another surgery, more radiation, and chemotherapy. It was a long, hard battle, but she did go into remission again.

As a little girl, I didn't fully appreciate that every time the cancer came back, it was more and more dangerous. I accepted it was an ongoing pattern and assumed she would always get better.

One afternoon, while my mom was resting in bed, I went into her room and asked if she would iron my pants for a school event the next day. This was back when clothing had to be ironed because fabrics were not yet wrinkle-free, and it was unacceptable to wear wrinkled clothing for a special event. She happily agreed to iron the pants and started to climb out of bed.

My grandmother was visiting us that day and overheard my request. She flew into the room and ordered my mother to stay in bed. She grabbed me by the wrist and yelled, "How dare you be so selfish? Can't you see your mother isn't feeling well? And why don't you know how to iron your own pants?"

Maybe, subconsciously, I thought my mom needed an activity to distract her from her pain. Or perhaps I didn't want to go to school with wrinkled pants. Or maybe I was afraid of burning myself with the iron. Or possibly all the above.

But that was the day my grandmother taught me how

to iron, and that was also the day I became afraid of asking for help.

Yup. Two lessons in one fell swoop. One good. One bad.

What I didn't know at the time was that my grandmother was suffering too. My mother, her daughter, had cancer, and my grandmother was afraid that my mother was dying. But I didn't know that—at least not the dying part.

My mom passed away a few months later.

As an adult, I understand this from both sides now. But then, that message became the source of "faulty wiring" in my brain.

I was already an overthinker and a people-pleaser, but now someone had thrown gasoline on the fire. I developed a reluctance to asking for help—and worse, admitting that I didn't know how to do something and needed help.

I loved my mother more than anything in the world. The thought of burdening her or acting selfishly was the worst thing I could have ever imagined. My embarrassment, humiliation, and profound guilt created a lifetime of trauma for me. And no matter how many decades have passed since that seemingly innocuous event, it still gives me a lump in my throat to talk about it or even write about it.

Decades later, when I was working with my first executive coach, she asked me why I had so much trouble asking for help in all aspects of my life.

It had never really occurred to me. I accepted that I was inherently wired to be hyper-vigilant, hyper-independent, and always act like the adult in the room.

This was when she introduced me to the concept of my *inner critic*.

Your inner critic refers to that voice inside you that judges, criticizes, or demeans you, whether the self-criticism is objectively justified or not. Mine sounds like this: "Don't be selfish. Don't be ungrateful. Don't ask for help. Don't burden others."

"Don't be greedy."

When an adult is trying to manage their suffering from substance abuse, mental illness, chronic pain, or grief, they can negatively impact others in the process. This is how adults unintentionally influence a lifetime trait for a child.

In the previous chapter on people-pleasing, I talked about how many of my clients were victims of parents suffering from one or more of these issues.

As adults, those who have experienced trauma in childhood often feel a strong urge to prioritize others over themselves—a result of their inner critic's voice.

Here's the good news: You're not stuck with your inner critic living rent-free in your head forever. You have the opportunity to rewrite your story going forward, even if the real-life source of your inner critic is still alive and well. Here are the steps to quiet the inner critic who lives inside you.

1. CREATE AN AVATAR

If you prefer to envision the actual person who inspired your inner critic (for example, I could have pictured my grandmother as the voice of my inner critic), that's fine. But if you want to have some distance from the actual person, you might want to find a character or a symbol or something that feels more benign.

My inner critic's avatar is Ursula, the sea witch from *The Little Mermaid* movie. Ursula is a charismatic antagonist determined to steal the little mermaid's beautiful voice. This avatar felt more acceptable to me than villainizing my grandmother, who was trying to manage her own grief.

My grandmother had survived breast cancer thirty years before my mother was diagnosed with it. She had also lost her own mother to cancer when she was a teenager. My grandmother was going through a range of emotions, including survivor's guilt and the painful memory of losing her own mother as a child. It was probably hard for her to deal with the idea of losing her daughter, and unfortunately, I got caught up in the middle of it all.

2. WRITE THEM A LETTER, BUT DON'T SEND IT

Tell your inner critic everything you have experienced and felt and what it has cost you. This letter can be as short or long as needed, but get it all out. Don't censor your thoughts, feelings, or word choice. Don't edit the first draft. This is your platform to feel safe, because you're not sending this letter. This is just for you.

When you finish it, edit it (or not), read it out loud, then shred it or burn it.

Over the years, I have found this exercise to be very powerful. It silences my inner critic and allows me to explore my feelings for those who have hurt me in the past.

3. TRY THE VOICE DIALOGUE TECHNIQUE

Drs. Hal and Sidra Stone created this tool in the early seventies. The exercise is designed to bridge the gap between yourself and your inner critic that lives in your subconscious.

Usually, it is done with the help of a facilitator—a counselor, therapist, or coach—but you can do it on your own. You begin by setting an intention for the session, and then you divide the conversation between your conscious and subconscious mind.

You may be dealing with your inner critic regarding a specific matter.

For example, if you struggle to lose weight, a version of you might be unconsciously holding onto the excess weight. Perhaps your inner critic is invested in you being thinner, and you're unconsciously rebelling against that voice. These are the questions to ask yourself in this exercise:

- What would your inner critic like to say to you?
- What would you like to say to your inner critic?
- What does your inner critic *need* from you?
- What do you *need* from your inner critic?
- What does your inner critic want to give you?
- What do you want to give to your inner critic?

Repeat all the questions two or three times to ensure you get the real answers. You can either write them down or record your voice. If you're doing this without a facilitator or counselor, it is best to record your questions and answers so you can stay present rather than having to worry about writing it down.

Once again, you don't need to confront your inner critic or the person who hurt you. They don't even need to be a living person.

At the end of this exercise, imagine two symbols: one representing you and one representing your inner critic. Choose two objects from the same category, such as animals, shapes, or colors. For example, you might choose a dog to represent you and a cow to represent your inner critic. Imagine each symbol in the palm of your hand. Then, bring your hands together in a prayer position, and with your eyes closed, take a moment to reflect.

Open your eyes and breathe. You might notice a sensation in your hands or body or a shift in your energy. The idea behind these two objects coming together is integration in whatever way it is perceived.

The key to understanding someone who has hurt you is that it's not about *you, even if it happened* to *you.*

When someone criticizes you, they are talking into a mirror. They are revealing something they fear or are afraid to admit about themselves.

Imagine your inner critic avatar (or the actual person) saying the exact hurtful words that haunt you. Then, imagine them saying it to their reflection in the mirror rather than to you.

4. PRACTICE FORGIVENESS

I finally understood that my grandmother was not trying to hurt me, humiliate me, or make me feel guilty. She was just scared, and her grief got misdirected toward me.
I have forgiven her for that.

Meditation is an excellent tool for practicing forgiveness. There are many guided meditations for forgiveness. My favorite is the Hawaiian prayer called Ho'oponopono. It goes like this:

I am sorry.
Please forgive me.
Thank you.
I love you.

Repeat this as many times as you need, silently or aloud.

If you struggle with using this prayer for someone who hurt you, then try offering it to yourself.

Forgiveness is the key to freedom. I have used this prayer hundreds of times and learned that forgiving others is powerful, but the real power lies in forgiving ourselves. When we practice forgiveness, we also practice self-compassion, and this is the first step toward self-love.

Loving yourself is not narcissism. It is self-care, and self-care is not selfish.

When you learn to quiet your inner critic, you free yourself from its shackles, and it no longer runs your show. Take your voice back, Ariel, and let Ursula the sea witch slither to the bottom of the ocean where she belongs.

Then, my friend, you're free to soar.

CHAPTER 11

Learning to Reframe Your Thoughts

When I became a life coach, one of the most valuable things I learned was how to manage my mind when challenging situations arose.

Humans love to assume that our thoughts are facts, particularly negative ones. When we have a negative thought, looking for evidence to support it is natural. Once we find evidence, that becomes a magnet for another negative thought. And before you know it, you're in a negative thought loop. This is another example of negativity bias.

There's a tool based on a cognitive behavioral therapy technique that teaches us how to reframe our thoughts and break free from negative thought patterns.

Everything in life is just a series of situations: birth, death, health, love, jobs, money, children, travel, friendships. When a situation arises, we automatically have unconscious thoughts about it, creating an emotional response in our bodies.

When we're in a spiral of negative thoughts, we can feel stuck or helpless. The goal is to challenge the thoughts to change the energy around those emotions. From there, we can process things differently to make a shift.

I call this doing your STEPS.

I'm not talking about the 10,000 steps recommended on your Fitbit or Apple Watch but the acronym for reframing your thoughts—STEPS.

S = Situation (Identify the issue)

T = Thoughts (List all your thoughts related to the issue that come to mind)

E = Emotions (Name one- or two-word adjectives to describe your emotions)

P = Process (Answer the question: What are you likely to do next?)

S = Shift (Answer the question: What is the likely outcome?)

Here's an example of using your STEPS.

I had a client who was a very religious man but was in a toxic and loveless marriage. He and his wife had been married for twenty years and had three children.

When he came to me, he was suffering from terrible anxiety. Despite having a successful career and being the primary breadwinner, he felt like a stranger in his own home. When he got home from work, he ate dinner alone.

He went to church on Sundays alone.

When he started working with me, he said that he needed help. He was in marriage counseling, but things seemed to be getting worse. He was unsure what to do, but he told me in our first conversation, "Divorce is not an option."

I simply asked, "Why not?"

He explained that because he was a deeply religious man, divorce conflicted with his values and his religion. We did a lot of work on his self-care and mindset, and I introduced him to the STEPS tool for reframing his thoughts. This is what it looked like for him:

Situation:	My marriage.
Thoughts:	It's terrible.
	My wife hates me.
	We have not been intimate in years.
	My children don't talk to me.
	It's uncomfortable to be at home.
	I eat dinner alone.
	I cannot get divorced.
	My community will judge me.
	My priest will not approve.
	I will be alone.
	I won't have a home.
Emotions:	Lonely. Trapped. Sad. Anxious.
Process:	Tolerate my current existence.
Shift:	Nothing changes. Feel lonely in my own home.

This was his subconscious version; it was all generated by his visceral thoughts and emotions.

So we did the exercise again with full awareness. The situation hadn't changed, but he had to look for thoughts that were neutral or positive about what could be possible.

SITUATION:	My marriage.
THOUGHTS:	I'm entitled to be happy. My family is entitled to be happy. I might be happier on my own. Life is too short to be miserable. I love my work, sports, and my religious community. I am capable of giving and receiving love.
EMOTIONS:	Hopeful. Curious.
PROCESS:	Talk to my religious leader. Continue marriage counseling. Hire a coach. Journal my feelings. Start practicing self-care. Choose happiness. Leave my marriage, if necessary.
SHIFT:	Make new friends. Develop hobbies. Find love again.

After listing the actions in the process step, he followed them as planned. He had a conversation with his priest, who recognized he had made every possible effort to save his marriage. Finally, the priest gave his approval to file for divorce.

My client moved into an apartment, learned to cook, made new friends, and hosted dinner parties. His children reconnected with him and developed new bonds. His business continued to prosper, and he found happiness again.

When you challenge yourself to think differently, you can create a different emotional response. When the emotions change, the process appears.

And that's when the magic happens! You discover a shift from reframing your thoughts!

Another client was facing issues with her weight, which she had been wrestling with for several years. She had gained forty pounds after giving birth and subsequently got divorced. Despite trying different diets, none of them worked.

We used the STEPS tool to first analyze the thought process behind her weight issues:

SITUATION:	My weight
THOUGHTS:	It's protecting me.
	It keeps me from dating.
	It helps me justify rejection.
	It is my punishment for having fled a toxic relationship.
	I don't deserve to be free.
	I'm afraid to be hurt again.

EMOTIONS:	Avoidance. Fear. Guilt.
PROCESS:	Eat junk food. Avoid exercising. Avoid dating.
SHIFT:	Nothing. Continue to carry forty extra pounds. No love life.

Then, we challenged her thoughts and did the exercise again.

SITUATION:	My weight.
THOUGHTS:	It *was* protecting me, but it no longer does. My weight is a scar left from some childhood trauma. My body no longer needs this excess weight. I can let it go now. My weight is holding me back from enjoying my new life. I eat to self-soothe.
EMOTIONS:	Liberated. Free. Hopeful.
PROCESS:	Start exercising daily. Track my food. Meal prep. Eliminate sugar and flour.
SHIFT:	Lose weight. Feel better. Regain my confidence.

This client believed that her obesity was similar to chronic pain. It gave her a constant excuse to avoid making plans and protected her from rejection. If she was rejected, she could assume it was because of her weight rather than her as a person.

Learning to reframe one's thoughts is another daily practice. However, it can be challenging for many people because we become attached to our thought patterns.

We forget that our thoughts are not facts.

We have to catch ourselves and recognize that thoughts are just thoughts. We have the power to retrain our brains to think differently. At the risk of sounding like a broken record, I am going to repeat: *This is a practice.*

If your perfectionism is getting in the way of you trying this exercise because you fear you won't do it perfectly, then remind your inner perfectionist: Practice makes perfect.

CHAPTER 12

Curiosity

In the previous chapter, I showed you how every *situation* is influenced by your *thoughts* and *emotions*, which creates your ability to *process* and make a *shift* in your life.

When I first learned to use this exercise to reframe my thoughts, my go-to emotion was usually "excited."

However, one of my coaches pointed out that while excitement is an emotion, it tends to be transient. In other words, when we get excited, we might jump into a new process, which might not be long-lasting. While I could argue that all thoughts and emotions are transient, "excited" tends to act more like a burst of energy than sustainable fuel.

After using the STEPS tool for several years, I have found a more sustainable and long-lasting emotion that feels grounded and powerful. One of my favorite emotions is *curiosity*.

Curiosity creates a sense of lightness and openness. It transforms us into investigators, students, researchers, interviewers, and explorers, making us more receptive to what's possible. Perfectionists often engage in black-or-white or all-or-nothing thinking. However, practicing curiosity can help counteract such thought patterns, especially when we face judgment from others.

We can avoid spiraling into negative thoughts by a snarky comment when we stay curious and neutral. One example might sound like this:

- Judgmental/negative comment: "You're always so forgetful."
- Curious/neutral response: Rather than getting defensive or snapping back, you can stay curious and say, "I can be at times. What strategies do you use to stay organized and remember things?"

You can defuse the situation quickly by acknowledging the comment without getting defensive. Then, when you redirect the conversation with an innocent question, the accuser is left with no option but to assume the role of teacher or expert.

When we get defensive or internalize negative comments, we can overthink and blow things out of proportion. I have spent many nights regretting conversations and wishing I had said or done things differently. But by staying curious, we can avoid making mountains out of molehills. Learning to reframe my thoughts has helped me overcome the habit of catastrophizing.

Overthinkers, people-pleasers, and perfectionists fear being vulnerable, needy, or ignorant about something. Hello, imposter syndrome! Imposter syndrome is the nagging feeling you're just winging it and haven't earned your achievements.

Imposter syndrome can make us feel like we don't deserve our accomplishments and that we will be exposed as frauds. To compensate for these feelings, we may overdo, overcommit, and overdeliver. We may also avoid asking questions or being curious out of fear of appearing ignorant.

However, curiosity is not a sign of ignorance but rather an act of bravery, integrity, and transparency. Being curious can help us learn and grow, liberating us from self-punishment and assumptions about how others perceive us.

For example, I've worked with many Hollywood screenwriters who struggle with receiving notes from executives and producers.

Writers can feel very vulnerable when they finally turn in their work. They often feel demoralized when their material is not met with adoration or glowing reviews. The critical notes can send them into a fight-or-flight state. They might feel misunderstood and want to give up.

When their creation is met with criticism, constructive or not, it can feel personal, as if someone is rejecting their baby.

When we stay curious, we stay out of the fight-or-flight mode, which means we listen better and think more clearly. Here is an example of a client using the STEPS tool to reframe his thoughts after getting notes on a script.

We ran through the exercise again with the intention of finding more neutral or positive thoughts.

SITUATION:	My script.
THOUGHTS:	There are so many notes. They don't like it. Why don't they acknowledge how hard I worked on this? Maybe I've lost my ability to write. Maybe I should find a new career. Maybe I'm not as good as I think I am. Maybe I'll get fired. Maybe I'll never work again.
EMOTIONS:	Fear. Embarrassment. Overwhelmed.
PROCESS:	Panic. Hide. Spin. Eat poorly. Skip exercising. Avoid writing.
SHIFT:	Feel terrible. The script doesn't get made. No income.

(Side note: After using this tool, my client found a great collaborator to improve their project dramatically.)

SITUATION:	My script.
THOUGHTS:	We all want the same thing—a hit show. The executives and producers are nervous too. They aren't writers, so they don't always know what to say. They're doing their best to articulate their concerns. They are rooting for me to succeed. My success makes them successful. We are all on the same team.

EMOTIONS:	Curious.
PROCESS:	Ask more questions. Stay neutral. Don't take notes personally. Offer to collaborate. Ask for help. Find another writer to collaborate with.
SHIFT:	Feel empowered. Motivated to solve the puzzle. Keep working. Improve the script.

Curiosity is a powerful emotion that can help us become better problem-solvers and collaborators and prevent us from spiraling.

So, when using your STEPS tool to reframe your thoughts, try aiming for the emotion of curiosity. It might be the ticket to finding a different thought and shifting your energy toward a more positive outcome.

CHAPTER 13

Asking for Help

As mentioned earlier, people-pleasers find it challenging to ask for help. They often see themselves as the person who always cares for others without realizing they need help. As a result, they may have never learned how to ask for assistance effectively, delegate tasks, or say no.

This behavior can lead to misunderstandings in their relationships with loved ones, who may not be aware that a people-pleaser needs help because they assume he or she has everything under control.

As adults, individuals who tend to please others may hesitate to ask for assistance. They've always made their own bed, literally and figuratively, so why would anyone lend a hand with their metaphorical fitted sheets?

When I ask clients why they're afraid to ask for help, the most common answers are:

"I don't want to bother anyone."

"Even if I ask for help, I'll end up doing it myself."

"They won't do it right." (Hello, perfectionist!)

"It takes me more time to ask them, remind them, and then show them how to do it."

These thoughts and emotions are rooted in fear:

- Fear of rejection
- Fear of nagging
- Fear of being needy
- Fear of being weak
- Fear of not being useful

The need to be "needed" becomes so powerful for a people-pleaser that it trumps their need to be helped.

How is that for a crazy circle of confusion?

I once had a therapist tell me that no one offered to help me because I didn't practice asking often enough. She told me, "You cannot ask for help setting the table or unloading the dishwasher one time and then stop asking when it's met with resistance or not done to your standards."

People can sense when we are reluctant to ask for help, and they learn that we will take care of things if they protest or wait long enough. So how do we break that cycle?

- Keep asking. Keep practicing.
- Prepare yourself for pushback.
- Expect that it'll be uncomfortable to ask for help.
- Know that it might be met with resistance.
- Understand that it may take longer than you'd like.
- Accept that the task may not be done to your standards.

You need to train yourself to use your voice to ask for things and retrain the people around you to listen.

Some will be happy to help, and others will be resistant. It's all right, but you need to be willing to endure some discomfort.

This is not about them. This is about you.

When you start caring for yourself, others will begin caring for you too!

When they see you make yourself a priority, they will also start making you a priority.

I had a client who was a working mother of three children, and her husband traveled a lot. She was the wife, mom, dog walker, cook, driver, housekeeper, *and* ran her own business. Her husband and her three teenage sons had no problem asking for things, and she was usually happy to oblige.

Until her health started to fail.

It began with fibromyalgia and then other autoimmune disorders. She knew that her illnesses came from exhaustion and sublimating her emotions. She began to gain weight, stopped exercising, lost interest in sex, and always felt tired.

She had very little joy left in her life.

When we started working together, I gave her weekly homework for self-care and encouraged her to ask her family for help daily.

She was very uncomfortable at first. Her teenagers were annoyed, and her husband only wanted to do things at his own leisure. She started asking for help with more authority and attached a timeline to her requests.

Within less than a week, everyone was helping more.

She noticed her chronic headaches started to subside, and her fatigue got better too. She couldn't believe the difference in such a short time.

It also changed the dynamics in her marriage. As a couple, she and her husband were much more engaged with each other and found themselves planning more alone time: date nights, time to exercise together, and long weekends away.

All because she was willing to ask for help.

I tell my clients to start with small requests but practice them daily. Regardless of the outcome, give yourself a gold star whenever you ask for something. Make it a game at first. Rack up the gold stars until it becomes a habit, and then see what other positive shifts occur simply by asking for assistance.

CHAPTER 14

The Power of Choice

Do you remember old-fashioned Chinese restaurants? They were my favorite growing up. Every Sunday night, my parents took us out for Chinese food, where we sat in big red vinyl booths and ordered Shirley Temples with little umbrellas.

The waiter would hand us thick, cushioned menus, and we would scan them to find our favorite dishes. There was always a family-style option on the menu:

- Egg Rolls or Fried Wontons
- Egg Drop or Hot and Sour Soup
- Fried Rice or White Rice
- Sweet and Sour Beef, Chicken, or Pork

Everyone loves a Chinese menu. Not just because Chinese food is delicious but because it gives us *choices*.

When we feel stuck in some aspect of our lives,

remembering that we have choices is our way to take back our power, even when things seem hopeless—like a job we hate, a relationship that has gone sideways, a financial hardship, or a health crisis.

We always have choices!

At times, when we're stuck, it can feel like our circumstances are bigger than we are. It seems like someone or something else is pulling the levers of our lives.

But we are not puppets. We are the captains of our own ships.

I had a client who held a prestigious executive job in Hollywood. She was earning a good salary, had a lot of visibility, and managed a large staff, but her workload was insane, and her bosses were difficult. Her demanding schedule, lack of autonomy, and aggravation at being constantly micromanaged frustrated her beyond description.

She was suffering from insomnia, weight gain, and elevated blood pressure, and her anxiety was through the roof.

She was miserable.

She had given up her power by believing she was a victim of her situation because she forgot to remember that she still had choices.

- She could discuss her feelings with her bosses.
- She could delegate.
- She could ask for help.
- She could set boundaries.
- She could choose to look for another job.
- She could save money and take a hiatus from working.
- She could change careers.

When we remember we have choices, we show up differently. We stop acting like victims and become superheroes of our own story.

It is essential to take inventory of your situation. What's working and what isn't?

This might run the gamut of your financial standing, social status, purpose in life, passions, career opportunities, reputation, safety, and comfort level. Once you have identified the areas that need improvement, you need to decide whether it's worth pursuing a change. If you do, then you need to determine how long you're willing to tolerate your current situation before taking action to make those necessary changes.

What small changes can you make right now to make it easier or better?

When I decided to leave the television industry, I had to create a financial plan to save enough money to make a career switch. Having a set deadline for my exit plan changed my perspective on my job. I could see the light at the end of the tunnel. Suddenly, the heavy workload and the challenging bosses became less burdensome. I started enjoying my work again because I knew it was finite.

In our relationships, it is also essential to challenge the status quo. We often avoid expressing our needs or setting boundaries for fear of upsetting the other person or damaging the relationship. While we don't want to be careless or hurtful, we need to be able to communicate honestly about our needs. Only then can we build healthy, fulfilling relationships based on mutual respect and understanding.

I had a client who was a mother of four with a full-time job, and she was feeling like a Burned-Out Betty. She juggled her children's needs, shuttling them to and from school and their after-school activities while working full time. Her weekends were spent at soccer matches, Little League games, gymnastics competitions, swim meets, and birthday parties.

Her husband, who also worked full time, was a good dad. However, he did not participate in the lunch-making, carpooling, or birthday party obligations. He traveled a lot for work and was a competitive triathlete, so he spent weekends training or competing.

When the client came to work with me, she was exhausted and overwhelmed. She felt like she had no breathing room, no time for self-care, and no release valve.

During our sessions, we talked about choices. She didn't feel like she had any. I reminded her that that was just a thought, because we always have choices.

We discussed her decisions to get married, start a family, and pursue a career. She acknowledged that she had willingly made all those choices but had not anticipated feeling so overwhelmed by their reality.

I asked her what she needed. She said, "Some time alone or with my sister, having a spa day or a girls' weekend." But she thought it was impossible because her husband would never take care of the kids by himself, and he would be burdened by her asking.

I reminded her that she worked and earned money and that having four children was a mutual decision. So why was she left in charge of managing everything? I told her that it was okay to express her needs and desires. Her homework was to schedule time alone with her husband to discuss her feelings—the burnout, the overwhelm, and the exhaustion. Initially, he was defensive, but he ultimately listened and asked how he could help. She told him she wanted to spend a weekend with her sister and have some quiet time.

And that's precisely what she did. When she returned home from her weekend away, she felt re-energized and grateful. Meanwhile, her husband developed a new appreciation for everything she did daily. The best part is that it improved their relationship. She felt more comfortable communicating with him, he became more hands-on, and she learned to take more time for herself.

We often forget we have choices when our people-pleasing habit is a well-worn neural pathway. People-pleasers don't want others to be inconvenienced or upset with them, so they bury their needs and forget they have choices. So, it starts with boundaries, and then we figure out what choices we have and what choices we're making.

Just like the Chinese menu, this is how we take back our power and get back to enjoying our lives.

I'll have an egg roll with that, please.

CHAPTER 15

Manifestation

Well, if you made it this far, congratulations! You're almost finished . . . at least with the book.

But before you go, we have one more critical step. It's time to dream big. It's time to start creating the life you want and not just surviving the one you have. It's about stepping into the world of possibility and learning how to manifest it.

Manifestation is bringing something into reality through thoughts, beliefs, and actions.

If you have trouble manifesting your goals and dreams, you're likely being blocked by some limiting beliefs.

Limiting beliefs are the stories we tell ourselves.

Whether it's your career, romantic life, money, weight loss, well-being, or friendships, these parts of your life are all vulnerable to limiting beliefs.

Earning money or having money is one of the most common goals thwarted by hidden thoughts. Some of the most common limiting beliefs around money sound like this:

- "I didn't grow up with money—therefore, I can never be rich."
- "I'm not good with money—so what's the point of having it?"
- "I know how to make money—but I'm bad at holding on to it."
- "More money, more problems—and I don't want more problems."
- "Money is the root of all evil—and I don't want money to corrupt me."

Whether you saw, read, heard, or were taught these beliefs, they can seep into your psyche and unconsciously sabotage your money goals or desires.

Or maybe money isn't your issue. Perhaps you struggle with finding the right romantic partner. Limiting beliefs can sabotage that goal, too, with thoughts like the following:

- "I've been hurt in the past, and I'm afraid of being hurt again."
- "I'm overweight."
- "I'm afraid of being rejected."
- "I'm not pretty enough."
- "I'm married to my job."
- "I don't have time for a relationship."
- "I'm too old to find love."

Or maybe money and romance aren't your issues, but you struggle with a lack of well-being. Thoughts like these might be getting in your way:

- "I have an autoimmune disorder, so I can never feel normal."
- "I had a car accident, so I have a lot of limitations."
- "I have fibromyalgia, so I never know if I'll have enough energy to show up."
- "I have allergies or asthma, so I'm limited in what I can do."

These thoughts are all limiting beliefs that might keep you from living your best life.

How can we differentiate the stories we tell ourselves from facts, and how can we debunk them?

1. BECOME A DETECTIVE OF YOUR TRUTH. IDENTIFY WHAT YOU WANT AND ASK YOURSELF WHY IT HASN'T HAPPENED YET.

What limiting beliefs are hindering your goals? Are they your beliefs or someone else's story? Be mindful of your inner critic and challenge it during this time.

2. WRITE DOWN WHAT YOU WANT. NOT JUST ONE THING BUT THE WHOLE ENCHILADA. THIS EXERCISE GOES BY MANY NAMES:

- My Ideal Life
- My Future Self
- My Personal Manifesto
- My Vision Statement

Call it whatever you like, but take a piece of paper, your journal, or your computer and start writing.

Pick a timeline for the future: six months, one year, or three years. I like the one-year date because it feels tangible and gives me enough time to start planning, but you decide what works for you.

I'm going to warn you now. Overthinkers, people-pleasers, and perfectionists tend to struggle with this exercise!

Overthinkers tend to overthink it.

People-pleasers tend to worry about what others will think.

Perfectionists won't start or finish it for fear that it isn't perfect.

Let's stop these three horsemen in their tracks.

When you do this exercise, I recommend using the Pomodoro writing technique. The method is just a few simple steps.

- Turn on whatever music motivates you, but without lyrics so you're not distracted.
- Set a timer for twenty-five minutes.
- Start writing in the present tense about where you will be in the future in the period that you picked (six months, one year, three years).
- Don't edit.
- Don't stop.

- Don't allow for interruptions.
- Just write.

You can take a five-minute break and set another timer for another twenty-five minutes if needed. Include as much detail as possible.

- Where do you live? In a city? In the country?
- What's your home like?
- What kind of work do you do?
- Who do you live with?
- What do you look like?
- What kind of car do you drive?
- What kind of clothes do you wear?
- Who do you hang out with?
- What do you do in your leisure time?
- How much do you earn?
- What trips are you planning?
- Whatever else you want to include.

Write everything in the present tense. Don't worry about how you get there. Anything is possible. This is your *future self*. This is your manifesto. Once your list is complete, keep it somewhere you can see and read it often.

Now, what steps must you take to get the ball rolling? You don't have to figure out the big steps, just a few small ones.

Now that you know where you want to be, you can use this as the filter for the choices you make in your everyday life. For example, if you want to change careers, you might need to start talking to people in the field that interests you, revise your résumé, or update your LinkedIn profile.

To lose weight, you might skip the fast-food drive-thru today, order a healthy salad, and start drinking more water.

If your goal is to quit drinking, maybe you attend your first AA meeting. Or call someone you know who gave up alcohol too.

If you dream of owning a home, perhaps you open a dedicated savings account and put money away for a down payment.

If you want to improve your physical fitness, you could consider walking a mile today.

The biggest mistake people make when making big plans is overwhelming themselves with the big steps.

"Dripping water hollows out a stone" is an apt metaphor for this. Sustained and consistent effort brings about noteworthy changes over an extended period.

The first time I did this exercise, here's what I wrote:

I live in a beautiful home with lots of windows.

I work from home.

My home office overlooks a garden and a swimming pool.

I write.

I help others through my writing.

I wear comfortable clothing.

I have no boss.

I make a good living, and I no longer have financial stress.

My husband is my best friend.

But here is what my life actually looked like at that time:

I was working in Hollywood for a huge corporation.

I wore formal clothes and impossibly uncomfortable high heels.

I had a very unpredictable, micromanaging boss.

I was in an unhappy marriage.

I had substantial financial pressure as the primary breadwinner and virtually no savings.

When I first had my dream, I didn't know how to make it a reality and become my future self. But by writing it down, I took the first step to bring it into existence.

Now, twenty-two years later, I live in Maui.

I am a life coach.

I love my career.

I am my own boss.

I work from home.

I wear comfortable clothes.

I no longer have debt or financial stress.

My home office looks out to a beautiful garden and a swimming pool.

I write daily—blog posts and podcasts, and now I'm writing this book.

I have been happily married to my second husband for the last twenty years.

It didn't happen overnight, but it did happen with baby steps.

I would love to tell you everything changed when I started paying attention to my hydration all day.

Or when I started focusing on eating protein at every meal and reducing my white flour and sugar intake.

Or when I learned to meditate.

Or when I took up tennis and found a hobby that I love and a workout that doesn't feel like exercise.

Or when I started journaling and had a place to put all my overthinking thoughts and emotions.

Or when I started tidying up daily, so my home always feels peaceful and uncluttered.

But it wasn't one thing. It was all the things, and with each step, I felt more confident, grounded, and grateful.

These changes started with baby steps, and then I practiced them until they became habits.

That's not to say I never have sad or bad days anymore. I still have to hip-check my people-pleasing tendencies, silence my inner critic, and throw a blanket over my overthinking perfectionism. But overall, it's gotten so much better because of the tools I have outlined in this book. As for my anxiety, it's now an occasional visitor instead of a permanent resident living in my body.

I remain a perpetual work in progress, but I'm proud to say that I built the life I no longer need a vacation from . . . and so can you.

One step at a time.

Practice, practice, practice!

ACKNOWLEDGMENTS

To my husband, Curt, for being the architect of my second act and my best friend. I so love and appreciate our life together.

To my daughters, Madison, Morgan, and Alexa, thank you for being my greatest cheerleaders. I am so proud of the fierce, independent, and loyal young women you have become. You all bring me such indescribable joy.

To my siblings—the tribal council. David, thank you for giving me my start in television and for everything you have done for me throughout my life. Debbie, thank you for inspiring me to become a coach and being the most loving sister. Greg, thank you for inspiring us to create our second act here in Hawaii.

To my team at KN Literary for holding my hand through the editing and publishing process.

To my clients who have entrusted me with their most profound challenges and vulnerabilities. You have been a source of inspiration for me and have impacted my own journey as well. Thank you for allowing me to walk alongside you and support you on your path.

Last but not least, to my office mate, constant companion, and best furry friend, Blaze. I appreciate you being by my side day and night and trying your best not to bark during my morning meditation and client sessions.

ABOUT THE AUTHOR

JACKIE DE CRINIS is a life coach who helps overthinkers, people-pleasers, and perfectionists manage their anxiety, be more productive, and happier.

Before becoming a life coach, Jackie spent over thirty years in the television industry as an executive for NBCUniversal, ABC, 20th Century Studios, and Sony Pictures Television Studios. She developed and oversaw dozens of Emmy and Golden Globe award-winning series as a creative executive.

In addition to her coaching practice, Jackie hosts *The Overthinker's Guide to Joy* podcast.

Jackie has three adult daughters and lives in Maui with her husband and dog. In her spare time, she plays tennis and pickleball, practices yoga and meditation, loves board games, and is learning to play golf.

If you would like to learn more, you can connect to Jackie at Jackiedecrinis.com

jackiedecrinis.com/podcast

INSTAGRAM: @jackiedecrinis

FACEBOOK: facebook.com/jackiedecrinislifecoach